TERRA FIRMA

TERRA FIRMA
Sacred Ground
POEMS • 1970–2022

MICHAEL MAGEE

MoonPath Press

Poetry
ISBN 978-1-936657-62-9

Cover art "Early Spring" by Uwe Arendt,
ArendtGraphics.com

Back cover author photo by Allen Braden
Interior author photo by Pat Scanlan

Book design by Tonya Namura, using Gentium Book Basic

MoonPath Press, an imprint of Concrete Wolf Poetry Series,
is dedicated to publishing the finest poets
living in the U.S. Pacific Northwest.

MoonPath Press
PO Box 445
Tillamook, OR 97141

MoonPathPress@gmail.com

http://MoonPathPress.com

*To J. Glenn Evans who introduced me
to my wife through poetry;
to the memory of
David Wagoner and Bill Matchett,
who taught me chapter and verse*

ACKNOWLEDGMENTS

Grateful acknowledgment to the publications that published many of the poems in this collection, sometimes in earlier versions.

10 Simple Pleasures: "My Socks, Martyrs to Lost Causes," "Nisqually Delta Without Birds"

A Trip to Jerusalem: "Limelight"

Anhinga Press, Cynthia Kahn 2nd Prize: "Mt. St. Helens, After the Fall"

Aria: "Like Irish Gardens in the Rain," "Night Mailman"

Bookends: A Poetic Memoir: "First Cousin," "Road to a Grecian Urn"

Calapooya Collage: "Dawn at Stonehenge War Memorial on the Columbia"

Clark Street Review: "Cathedral of Stone, the Sunshine Mine Disaster"

Dirt? Exhibition, University of Puget Sound: "At the Ginkgo Interpretive Center," "Follow Me"

Hopscotch (England): "Film Noir," "The Marionettes of Prague," "Slavia Café, Prague"

Hotchpotch: "At the Temple of the Glen, Iona," "Culloden Battlefield," "Minding the Gap," "My Phone Card from Marrakech"

In Tahoma's Shadow Anthology: "Found Object"

Jack Straw Writers Anthology: "At Peace on the Klickitat," "Pointless"

KING FM *Listener Tales*: "Voice in the Machine"

Medley: "Marked by a Palm"

Mélange: "Two Epigrams"

Music on the Strait.Com: "Korean Lullaby"

NineMuses: "Saturnalia," "Christmas at Lincoln, England"

The Nottingham Evening Post: "A Trip to Jerusalem"

Only Connect: "Tired Bodies," "R.S.V.P."

Perceptions: "Mdina, the Silent City," "Haġar Qim," "My Comings and Goings from Mosta"

Poetry Atlas.Com: "Deadwood, South Dakota"

Poetry (Chicago): "Murder Weapon," "Nightwatch"

Poetry Northwest: "The Circus," "Out of Season"

PoetsWest Literary Journal: "Arthur's Seat," "At Intermission (Not Tom Stoppard)," "Attrition," "Bedtime Story," "Main Attraction," "Sphinxes of the Grand Coulee," "Sarah Brightman and the Peacocks," "Star Quality"

Queen Anne News: "Coffee Has Taken Away the Songbirds"

Real Change: "I Am Not a Hunter Gatherer"

Riddled with Arrows: "Still Life"

Staxtes Greek Literary Journal: "The Windmills of Hydra"

CONTENTS

III.

HOLY LANDS
Mediterranean to the Black Sea

IV.
LIMELIGHT
Last Calls and Final Acts

V.
PILGRIMAGE
Scotland and England

TERRA FIRMA
Sacred Ground

*When someone asked Socrates of what country
he was he did not reply 'Of Athens' but 'Of the World.'
'If there is anything remarkable in his neighborhood
let him go see it, whether it is a building, a fountain,
a man, the site of an ancient battle, or a place visited
by Caesar or Charlemagne.'*
      —Michel de Montaigne,
        "On the Education of Children,"
        Collected Essays

SATURDAY MORNING

Light on the ground,
insects all around,
the glowing kale and pansies
wearing their circus faces,
Coleus with its open-mouthed petals.

I sit at an ornamental iron table
in the sun in late September,
the hum of heavy metal from buses,
trucks, the car wash merry-go-round
over the coffee machine's daily grind.

Sitting at the Cosmonaut Café
on the rooftop, walls like I was
at Sirkeci, a blue omniscient sky,
I hear the cry of the traffic muezzin
to worship the automobile

with its hood-ornament trophies
among the bubble and squeak of life,
talking like we were cicadas,
and filling in with the breeze
the frieze of the sky.

I.

LOCAL COLOR
Washington

Nuestro amor ha nacido   Our love was born
fuera de las paredes,   outside the walls,
en el viento,   in the wind,
en la noche,   in the night,
en la tierra   in the earth

—Pablo Neruda, *Epitalamio*

THE SHOELACES CRY TO BE UNTIED

"Unloose me, unloose me," they sing
"for we are the cobbler's children."
Threadbare, their finger ends dangling
pulling themselves into ribbons that hold
the beginnings of knots tied into secrets.

That are united into pretty bows, praying:
"Let us walk together or be parted." Oh,
for every foot that drags lamely behind,
for those who stumble, let them recover
by throwing off their tongue-tied bindings.

So others may walk flat-footed into the world,
pigeon-toed, strutting or striding, in a gait,
springing as the sole-masters of their fate,
rising from fallen arches poised and ready
to be counted among the barefoot elect!

FOLLOW ME

*The ground is covered by a layer of grit created
by tourists who have done nothing more vicious
than walk.*
    —*National Geographic*

Even in Ancient Ephesus
where each footprint said, "Follow me,"
it was the accepted way—

to follow the path, tracing their messages
a scrabble of letters like a Ouija board
in earth where men were easily led
to walk following in their footprints

finding women in loose-fitting garments
waiting—soft and willing.
Never in their serpentine ways would
they have dreamed we would come here.

As we try not to stray from the beaten path
to promises of *touch me* and *look here*
knowing there is nothing vicious in just
walking in another's footsteps.

DAWN AT STONEHENGE WAR MEMORIAL ON THE COLUMBIA

Amid Nature's Great unrest
He sought rest.
　　　—Sam Hill, *Epitaph*

Even before dawn, names had appeared in this stone
circle, on plaques cast in bronze, rock faces told of
Cro Magnon, before the Promethean fire came those
hunters of Orion's fame, before the wood gatherers
came our long-deceased fathers who used bow
and arrow to hunt their mythical stags, and now,
their sons are here on the eve of another hunting season,
when chuckers are driven into their holes, ducks shot at
for sport, and white-tailed deer seek cover in the forest,
these militiamen keep watch: the living over the dead.

Last night Orion's belt glittered, the North Star pointed
the way to the Big Dipper, the belly of the moon was full
with drinking as it tried to swallow us through Satus Pass.
We drove in a state of confusion, looking only for signs
reflected back to the town we knew existed on our maps.
Yakima gleamed as an alien city "Patrolled by aircraft,"
but we survived unnoticed, invisible to their radar screens,
although the army firing range lit up like a scoreboard.
They lost us, we drove on automatic pilot to get through.

At Stonehenge, the circle is closed, ringed by walnut trees,
dead fruit covers the ground, split open like magma
serving as stepping stones to overlook this wide Columbia
Gorge, while south across the river, Mt. Hood grows
to a mushroom, the dry wind sweeps down like a sword.
No hosannas here, or wreaths, only rattlesnakes hidden
away in cracks, waiting for the sun to blister the earth so
they, too, can sleep. Mesas fill out the view, terraces

layered in pink granite tell of a Coral Sea
with bodies spread out like anemone.

It took a Quaker pacifist to dream of such a resting place
for those war dead, tablets written with Roman numerals.
Those stars of our distant fathers faded into sunrise; when
we heard shots at daybreak we wondered was it reveille
for the buried here, like those deer soon to be slaughtered,
or some higher orders that made the guns echo target
practice. Nothing had changed, the old laws were still
obeyed in blood, human sacrifice kept sacred,
hunters and hunted born as one. We knew it was the same
with all men; it had always been.

SPHINXES OF THE GRAND COULEE

You were a riddle to me even as a boy,
fathoming Deep Lake was a mystery,
the curiosity of Electric City generating
toasters and television sets was a dream.
I expected shining stainless-steel towers,
fences humming with electricity, power lines
dusty mirages, walking the streets of town.

My mother tells of other times, Grand Coulee
was a boom town, wide-open twenty-four hours,
hootch everywhere, knee-deep in mud and bars
and women playing for keeps beneath the stars.
They built the dam, dismantled the town,
only the earth still shadows its remains,
the old Indian trails make question marks
where the Columbia has been damned into lakes.

Soap Lake's hope of healing waters disappears
as minerals leech out, returning to the clay.
Once it could hold a body afloat for days,
now the levitation of this natural miracle,
a therapeutic lake foams around the mouth
like a mad dog, sick to death, even of itself.
The health spas and baths are closing down
as people shift on toward the next oasis.

Promises crumble before blasted rocks,
hungry glaciers that changed a river's course
leave behind only these ruins of pothole lakes,
a waterfall wider than Niagara long gone dry.
Where it pales, the Devil's Punchbowl lives in spirits

of green groundwater turned to a brackish brew.
Amid sagebrush and rattlesnakes, Steamboat Rock
lies stranded without a river, waiting to rise again
on the next great post-diluvian shore.

AT THE GINKGO INTERPRETIVE CENTER

To remove plants, rocks, soil from here
is larceny, the sign says.
No ripping off of nature permitted
as the Ginkgo Center interprets it to us.

A visitor asks if any trees can still be seen,
while our guide points out two in front of us,
no leaves or branches on one side;
they grow against a wall of stone.

Looking at the Columbia Gorge, we see
layers of strata stripped away, sediment
stripes in red and brown, not these trees
with fragile fan like leaves.

These are the petrified forests, once
rooted in soil, only a few stumps left
to sit on. As a fossil, I wonder—
how well will I survive?

MT. ST. HELENS, AFTER THE FALL

There is winter everywhere
in the gray trees, shocked of their leaves,
bleached white as driftwood, incongruous
as an ocean beach to find trunks turned up
revealing their roots,
timber scattered like jackstraws, a valley
with nothing left to fill, but here and there
fireweed coming back to reclaim the groundwater

in bursts and patches of lupine, above bald hills
white as eagles' crowns showing through,
fringes of green where the gases cut like a scalpel,
a grove of trees like the shell of a cathedral
and surrounded by a fence, the burned-out miner's car
that has been hurled across the road,
flattened like a can, now serves as a planter
for grass growing up through the floorboard,
memorial to a family of three.

The bus might be climbing roads in Peru
in this Andes of devastation, finally arriving
at the outlook above Spirit Lake, which has risen
two hundred feet since the explosion
at one end, logs now thick as cattails that once
covered it before Harry Truman's lodge
vanished beneath the wake. Seven miles away
the mountain lies hidden beneath its weather,
while in the crater another lava dome is building.

Here, no consolation except Meta Lake,
protected by snow, an oasis giving birth to billions
of tadpoles, only the sounds of killdeer rise above
the stillness, while a few bees savor the desserts
of pollen left in wildflowers, this mountain's tarn

the only reminder that something made it through,
the terrible heat wave travelling across the land
leaving gray stone so light it will float on water.
Signs say leave the pumice where you found it;
then wait for the fireweed to return, and where death
leaves its fingerprints, please do not disturb.

I AM NOT A HUNTER-GATHERER

As the day begins:
an owl flutters
from beneath my eyelids,
lulled by the soft wind
beneath the stars,
out hunting for morsels
of cat and mouse.

It's still too early
for bigger prey.
I rustle from my foxhole
of sleep without a sheep
or a nose-twitching rabbit.
I sharpen my claws.

I've lost the scent,
face up to the clock,
admit: I am not
a good hunter-gatherer.
Second hands whirr
in the gamey dark.

NOVEL CORONAVIRUS

This morning a robin and a flicker
sat down together on the sidewalk

sharing the same grain, taking turns
while making room; then flying into

a tree, surveilling, then returning as
they do to make the best of it, as I

make my way to Thriftway to buy
toilet paper, dishwashing soap,

and find the shelves bare except
for two bottles (I only take one),

thinking of the robin and flicker who
share what little they have perfectly
happy to make a meal of what's left.

FOUND OBJECT

The raccoon looks soft as a kid glove
along the roadside, as if it had been sleeping
with its striped tail bowing on its prayer rug.

I wish I had fur as soft and beautiful as this
dusky fur and could steal away with such a coat,
cosmic looking as the great spiral nebula.

For its resting place looks peaceful, as though
it was making its way for the gully so full of glowing
clematis that it could take off its mask for once.

IN THE COWICHEE CANYON ROAD

Swerving around the horseshoe bends,
we rim the road, the hop fields
in the distance, filling up the frame.

We're bound for the trailhead, suddenly coming
to a turn-off onto the gravel where
two quail scurry across, ahead a dead end.

Find a house or two abandoned, a basketball hoop
where someone left his empty net,
but go no further; it's almost dark.

Three miles through the sagebrush
with rattlesnakes waiting on the rocks.
I imagine turkey vulture, red-tailed hawks,

American kestrel, yellow-breasted chat,
Bullock's oriole and whistling marmots
we leave for another time. The quail leave
their farewells in high-pitched squawks.

SKATECREEK CANYON ROAD

The man in the Railway Café at Elbe
  says rest your eyes, relax your heart,
    take in the soft Chinook wind

that blows across your arms
  bent in the elbow of this shadow that
    keeps reaching toward birch and alder.

Beyond the ski lodges and gift shops of Ashford,
  you take a right into the Guifford-Pinchot
    National Forest

as you follow the switchback roads
  on the moss side of your face,
    crisscrossing this river of sticks.

Above the scree of rock and earthslides,
  an avalanche turned up among the many
    waterfalls of sword fern and maidenhair.

Where clusters of Queen-Anne's lace appear
  for you, this road ends in a question mark
    answered only by whistling marmots.

A GLOSSY PHOTOGRAPH

As I look to your photograph in its frame
surrounded by black to make you shine,
I see in you a sheer white glacier wall—
your eyes reflect the stone granite
there as rockfall comes down the valley
but never touches you at all, my love.

So serene, you are smiling still though
death has become you, never broken, yet
your words are far away, a mountain's
range, Mt. Rainier among the Cascades.
Still you have the whitest smile that glows
at me from the window of my lens.

Yet you unbend the light to look straight at me,
holding up the snow around your rounded
shoulders that never made me look behind
to follow where you begin, my mountain's
waterfall stream of being. May you always be
the last piece of my living where you end.

FUNERAL MARCH

When your family gathered to say good-bye,
it was like an old photograph
dressed in mourning clothes,
the rite of men in black suits,
women in dark dresses
gathered at the graveside.

But we in our passage had just
come from Tacoma to Seattle
fresh from the D.O.T to get your
enhanced driver's license for a trip
over the border to Canada.
So, when we appeared it was
you in comfortable shoes,
and I in purple and blue.

Like a bouquet of outlandish
hydrangeas as though to lighten
the occasion, brought by a pair
of old vaudevillians there to recite
"Face on the Barroom Floor" from
memory (like my grandfather) when
a Chopin dirge was de rigueur.

FIRST COUSIN

for Don Lyons

In his living room a pillow says
"Screw the Golden Years," and a blanket
trumpets, "Custer Had it Coming."
"I take my bow for a walk in the woods,"
my cousin says, but only nails an odd grouse
and goes hiking with his weapons,
missing an Elk with his rifle,
then smokes the peace pipe.
The rifles he keeps are all unloaded.

The coved ceilings of his living room
harbor dream catchers that radiate
bigger than a spider web, and in the red
and white oak of his living room
floor sits his blind and deaf dog Maxwell.
"A true gentleman" inherited from a friend who
died. "You get the Dodge and the dog."

My cousin worked the railway bridge near Everett.
For Christmas, "I got a train, an erector set,
and ten little men who work half the time."
Then he retired, and a photo of Chief Kamiakin
looks on from the Yakama Tribe, a face
polished bright, Mt. Adams appears at his window.
On his refrigerator door he keeps a saying:
"Wag more and bark less!"

AT PEACE ON THE KLICKITAT

The photo of the model was taken in April;
she was murdered in October.

Yes, she seemed to fit
  angled on the steep slope,
a nude lying on her side.

Under the grove of trees
  but hanging on only by
the long roots of her hair.

Here may she rest
  so young and unaware,
uncovered by the fact

of her death while she
  still ripens at the loss,
vulnerable as fruit.

Her body in repose
  not yet starting the slide
that gravity takes,

far from the trees
  delivered inconveniently
from grace.

SCRIMSHAW ON LAKE CRESCENT

Written in rock faces at Lake Crescent,
tracings of seagulls' feet, veins
of our ancestors, American dippers
along the river and the shore
where we now dangle our feet
in silence, the Storm King nearby.

We take up residence, climb to
Marymere Falls, switchbacks
like a bridal train spilling out below,
then back through crumbling
cedar logs, red bricks of the forest.
Our words seem inconsequential.

Here, far from clearcut—
this forest with hemlock and Douglas fir
makes us listen to every little wing, while
back at the lake, enclosed by
steep sides in Vs, makes our eyes
widen with vision.

Still hoping to be seen, scrimshaw
written on the lens, today I am
indigenous as a poet with a lineage
going back to my pen. This morning
I wrote two poems in birdsong—
waiting for translation.

LAKE CRESCENT, LADY OF THE LAKE

The bundle retrieved by fishermen on July 6,
1940 turned out to be the body of a woman.
        —Mavis Amundson, *The Lady of the Lake*

At the end of my run of words
spilling down like Marymere Falls
in bridal trains.

A woman disappeared—
her resting place sends
shivers through me.

The silent ridges of Lake Crescent
600 feet deep, and Hallie Brooks Latham
tied up in ropes.

The waters must have run cold
for her, tied down
with her big fisheyes.

I set for the evening sun,
my brown skin wet,
looking out across the lake

for the lady who came
up one last time
to take a breath.

SUNDAY EVENING WITHOUT
WALLACE STEVENS

from the Riviera Hotel
in Port Angeles

This has been a shining afternoon
with sun on my sandwiched body—
lotion and tan—from my porch
by the winding semi-circular staircase.
As I turn the wheel around the corners
with this sun on my arm, bronzed,
a merry widower in my own waltz time,
a little dizzy, my day without a rhyme.

Looking at a peak coming through
the clouds, each page is another
turn and I am the captain without
my first mate, ghosts of the San Juans,
Lopez, and Friday Harbor, blue shadows,
and Field Hall, pillars of wood and glass.
Incoming currents, Ediz Spit sheltering
container cargo ships offshore,
poking out like a little finger.

The streets are named after our aunts:
Eunice, Caroline, Queen Victoria,
Georgiana, *wife of the above*, down
the street a veteran is sleeping at
the War Memorial, an I-beam
rooted in the ground from 9-11.
A seal suns itself on the rocks, and
nearby a mourning dove, while a man
is frozen on a rock like a homeless
version of the Little Mermaid.

The sand rife with human depressions,
little hollows carved out for modern-day
cave dwellers to lay their bedrolls in.
I sit on a decaying stump as the tide
makes its run, writing it down, and find
a gate to a hovel where I see a small foot
wrapped in an Indian blanket, bones
of a campfire long gone out, on the edge
of wild blackberries I pick one ripe, as a man
passes incongruous in a Santa Claus hat.

And yet, this was a fortified village,
of the Nez Perce encampment.
Then a pulp mill and the stack from Rayonier
still stands, as Ennis Creek empties out
into the Straits of Juan de Fuca.
Now the seagulls have a field day as
I walk in silence among spruce and alder
where no canoes are carved, a trail
of broken logs, a ghost town of
pulp fiction, waiting to see an Indian
come out of the woods, a black mop
of hair from Sekiu Sequim, 7 nations.

The sky is a long blue line across
to Vancouver Island, across the straits
where islands form an archipelago
of a necklace up Haro Strait,
and no one trades except for tourists
taking the Black Ball Ferry to Victoria,
with smokestacks like Raven gods.
A crowning sparrow, some sandpipers
leave hieroglyphs on the beach as a woman
walks in broken footprints.

NEW YEAR'S 2022

I went out with Leonard Cohen
and Neil Young, came in with Marianne
Faithfull and 20th Century Blues
walked in the slipstream of ice floes,
my fuzzy feet holding me up
in the snowdrifts, half-steps between.
My New Year's Eve march to
Radetzky March in old Vienna.

Wearing my Christmas green and black-capped
chickadee sweater with antlers hanging high and dry,
my Genghis Khan knit hat with the
Heidi braids, a half-crescent Covid mask
hanging like a used G-string from my neck.
Sherpa roots and sheepskin boots with
a "Moon River" grin wider than a mile
hoping I would smile some day.

Off I go at midnight to traverse
the distance between post holes
and telephone poles, no telephone
booths to ring the New Year from,
on reindeer tracks flashing the gap
between my front teeth where the implants
will go crossing a wide expanse—
anticipating a new forest to explore.

II.

R.S.V.P.
From Idaho to South Dakota

I don't know my location but my orientation...and likewise if they ask me what shape the world is, if they ask the self that dwells within me...the horizon is the only continuous line.

—Italo Calvino, *The Road to San Giovanni*

AT MINERAL

At the old town along the lake
a rusted train, like it came
from an old erector set,
and a "no trespassing" sign
at West Fork Timber.

At the grocery store there's
no public access to the restroom
but a woman comes in to buy
some oatmeal and a loaf of bread.
I give her 28 cents (she's just short).

The owner treats me to a cup
of coffee. "There's not many people
who would do that." "You either
do it or you don't," I say, and take
my coffee out to the porch.

Today there's an art show
and a place to put old clothes.
I walk to the picnic table
which doesn't have a website yet.
Songbirds fill the air.

Nearby, a collapsed house that
looks like a boulder sat on it
all ready for bulldozing, while along
the water people are cruising in
rubber boats big as landing craft.

I leave as I came, empty-handed.
The oldest man in town just

died from arsenic poisoning
after 98 years. Here they say, "Take
a little every day until you're dead."

CATHEDRAL OF STONE, THE SUNSHINE MINE DISASTER, KELLOGG, IDAHO, MAY 12, 1972

At the 1313 Café in Wallace, a yellowed-newspaper,
shows greased faces of the miners surrounded by
their families eight days after the dust had settled.
—Spokesman Review, May 10, 1972

Fire has sucked out the spirits of the dead
from the 4800-foot level, down where
the bitter drill has stopped, and oxygen
is guttering in mine shafts 10 and 12.

Their fighting spirit gone, eight days later,
Flory and Wilkinson recovered alive, 47 gone,
44 still remaining. Tears make a winding
chain of the families where men are still rising.

In blackout, goodness has been snuffed out
as the men worked against the darkness; now
their names are etched in dark stone. Look,
they shine in beams of daylight. All 91.

Men still come to this roadside monument,
the miner's headlamp is lit on his hard hat.
Ashes and grit hold them day and night
like the man who raises his diamond drill.

Still, my friend says, "If the price of silver
ever goes up again, on a bright day like today,
streams of water running out of the mine, hot as coffee,
the chain will start to wind in the headstocks again."

Maybe it will be time to go to work once more
down at the bottom of the pit where it's 138 degrees,

silver and copper will be sent to the smelters,
miners rising in black with their headlamps shining.

FROM GHOST TOWNS OF
NORTHERN CALIFORNIA

a guide

They all look lived-in once,
now like Roman ruins, walls
or old aqueducts.

Coloma, New Lotus, and Pilot Hill,
Placerville where the
Gold Bug struck.

In the Wah Hop Store herbs
"favored by Chinese argonauts"
still hang like old fossils.

The school once destroyed by a
runaway logging truck is rebuilt
and in perfect order.

Lotus once had 2000 souls
until the placer deposits ran out,
a sleepy town now dead as
the Uniontown cemetery.

At Pilot Hill, the elegant Bayley Mansion
lost its front porch and veranda,
and then its business when the railroad
bypassed it.

Next, Georgetown, called "growlersberg—
because nuggets growled in miner's pockets,"
the Stamp Mill where you'd like to go deaf.

Not any more; the dead aren't listening.
Go north to Reno, east to Lake Tahoe,
or further west to Sacramento, young man.

POETIC OUTLAWS

Without poets, without artists...everything would
fall apart into chaos.
　　　—Apollinaire

We wear masks to hide our identities,
go out in public, but stay incognito
while keeping our words to ourselves,
hidden, not picking a fight we can lose,

keep ourselves holstered, waiting for
the moment to pull out our pens in
privacy, as though we were desperadoes
in search of richer rewards. Banks are

not for us, or even safe deposit boxes.
Those we can blow with explosives.
The combinations are in our minds
and there's no safe we can't crack.

Savings and Loans mean nothing to us,
no Bonnie and Clydes, no strongarm
hold-ups, but instead we stay focused
using only our bare-knuckle words.

DEADWOOD

Burned out on the street corner,
the girl from the casino
having lost everything must
still go back to take her losses.

In Kevin Costner's Midnight Star
people go to photograph the photos
of *Bull Durham* and see the uniform
he wore in *Dancing with Wolves*.

We see Kevin the Bullsnake,
posing on a rusted cable box in the sun,
who came two weeks ago
and never left except for shade.

Brick streets of Deadwood,
long after Wild Bill Hickock met his match
buried up on the ridge along with Calamity Jane
still holding his *dead man's hand of Aces & 8s*.

Downtown, there's the Gold Dust Saloon
and Cadillac Gaming House
and a place where they re-enact
the trial of Jack McCall.

Meanwhile, Kevin the Bullsnake still lies
flat in the sun and Costner hasn't
been here since 2012, an absentee
landlord with a load of bankroll.

While those girls on the street corners
leftover from the brothels, gaming the house,
still walk the dead-end streets of town
like an episode from *Twilight Zone*.

SIMPLE PLEASURES FROM BURNET, TEXAS

for Lane Chisholm

I expected to open your letter to find salamanders' tails,
a snake rattle, the remnant of an armadillo's traces
moving across the blue horizon line of the page,
a night of blinking stars like strings of fiesta lights
hanging in ropes above my head, and hear thousands
of crickets chirping from the corners of the envelope.

Instead, your shiny photographs of the "rock ruin
of an old pioneer home, beautiful Lake Buchanan,
about the size of Lake Washington" and an enormous
oak tree in your yard, your hand rubbery as roots
greeting me, the joyous tears of your unsalted words,
from the shores of your own private beach,
as these pebbles make little waves of applause.

MILKWEED

for Leona

A dandelion in a glass,
a fragile heart gone
to a reflection after
its love has left it,
would be transparent as this
white-haired remnant, so
beautiful in its stillness,
its curved spine, space
between where air has passed
a snowy head like yours.

POINT NO POINT

Jennifer in the coffee shop
directs us with a *stimulus package*
$1 drip—to the third light.

Then we come to the names:
Idlenot Road, Eagle Point, Buck Lake,
toward the bird sanctuary at Foulweather Bluff.

Over the speed tables' backs
like humpback whales, past
the "deaf child area" sign.

Past the pilot house of the grounded
MV Jupiter where we look for
a few cars parked at the trailhead.

Past the single engine fire station
the end is near at last. We make it to
the entrance. "No clamming, fires or dogs."

Enter among the cedar, hemlock, fir,
flushing a downy woodpecker
out of the shadows, we finally reach

a rocky beach, in the distance the Floating
Hood Canal Bridge drifts on the tide, arching
its back to connect the Olympic Peninsula's dots.

You say the ferns are "taller than we are,"
shafts of light open, and our feet tread
softly as the sun begins to leave us—

At Point No Point Lighthouse
we see the mirage of a six-story cruise ship
steaming toward Alaska like a colossus.

A hydrofoil with its Union Jack flying
is roiling the waves, coming back from Victoria
a container cargo ship fills the inside passage.

Where the weather station's radar is tracking
incoming storms, we've reached our limit of words.
The evening casts its tides as we drift out.

MY FATHER'S DRIFTWOOD

Once it had been a lamp—
my father drilled a hole
ran a cord through it,
his offering of light,
shaped by his temper
it balanced on one side
like a stork.

After he died, I took it apart,
kept the driftwood,
never bothered sanding it,
this wood made his icon.

When I left for England
I took it to the beach,
left it on the sand
to be carried on a high tide.

Now I'm home again, finding
I don't fit the same as before.
I think of the man, unfinished
along this shore, wait for you
to drift back.

TIRED BODIES

People wonder where I've gone.
I say nights are too long,
the days too short.

People ask me *when will you*
make a living, what will
you do. I answer in half-tones,
make it up, don't wait for luck,
keep my hands tucked in
at my sides like penguins do.

I pull up the bedsheets,
I say words are watchful,
I'm working undercover,
love doesn't get any easier,
neither do poems,
like the washing, it gets done.

I find my inspiration
in this day by day making,
a blue jay sits outside in a tree
making songs, spreading joy.

What I string together
is like washing on the line, love
is how we find ourselves.

THE ART OF WASHING DISHES

Closely observed, the art of washing dishes
has a wonderful ring to it,
which makes tea ceremony seem absurd.

How beautifully you linger, run your
eye and hand over every blessed one,
how each one leaves its imprint.

Like cups and saucers, the mother duck
arranging her young, and in the sink
after rinsing is done, so much

squeezed from a wet sponge,
only your dishrag will dry the tears
left from the cold rims.

MY SOCKS, MARTYRS TO LOST CAUSES

Try to find each other
inside my drawer to mate,
the single argyle, the available
black, the ever-popular tan.

Why must they always wait
without lovers, a single destiny
while others find fulfillment
in each other's embrace.

It is always this way.
If they could be happy for once,
find another who is true to the spirit
of what it means to be a pair.

R.S.V.P.

I have come out of hiding,
pot-washer, sandwich picker,
birth child of a factory age.
I was the one who fed
       the production line.

A child of no particular famine,
I learned from poor relations.
My mother worked in a laundry,
my father, a gambler, who learned
       he couldn't win.

I became a belly-acher, left home
rather than face up to laundry.
I roamed back alleys, prowled docks,
passed hand to hand
       like a fiver.

Too young to know better,
old enough to remember, I was
the one who avoided the military,
I have yet to answer
       all those letters.

ROAD TRIP: KEYSTONE TO
THE KEY PENINSULA

There in South Dakota where there are cliffs
and canyons and thickets of ponderosa pine,
Here there are Douglas fir, birch and alder
where you come to the end of the road.

There the road goes straight across
the plains south towards Kansas.
Here, a "key" where you turn around in
a cul-de-sac before going back on a 2-laner.

There you find hay rolled in the field
like Indian prayer bundles at Devil's Tower.
Here there are stone cairns and
an old cemetery in Longbranch.

There, there is Pierre (Peer), Belle Fourches
(Beautiful Fork) and Leed (not "lead") and
Deadwood. *Here, Home Depot and Key Center*
and Longbranch founded in 1891.

There sweet clover enough to feed
all the horses and bees. *Here a*
meadow or two and firewood stacked
against the house for the Autumn.

There it's 20 below in winter and
in summer the din of the Cicadas
going off like smoke alarms. *Here,*
clamshells near the Purdy Spit.

Here apples and roadside turnouts
where I write this so I won't forget there—
a memory going back to the Black Hills.

THE ROAD

A dividing line is great
that separates comings and goings,
holding you in its adverse camber.
You always feel a whinger's hearbeat
pulling you faster toward the pace car.

The road will tease you into judging
a safe distance, always closing in, objects
in the mirror are closer than they look,
like children, who loom in your rear vision.
This is no freeway; it costs plenty.

These broken lines you try to follow
trail off in Doppler effects and darkness
may hold your attention, but never think
you can relax, there is no escape here,
only the lure of this tunnel vision.

Twig-hopping will get you nowhere, beyond
headlights you can't see the dangers.
Confidence makes you a back-seat driver
but may leave you out on a limb, never
knowing exactly where this road dead ends.

GOOSE COMMANDER C

First

I

follow

the

Goose

Commander

in

my

sleep

I

go

where

she

goes

tuck

myself

inside

her

left

wing

middle

from

down

step

half

one

note

a

like

myself

point

I

as

me

before

tailwind

the

ride

then

NISQUALLY DELTA WITHOUT BIRDS

Today the bullfrogs in their echo chambers hide
among the green algae and cattails sucking mud.
We hear nesting sounds in the marsh.
As we pass along the boardwalk, a flight
of Canada Geese rushes beneath radar
full of squawking, while a mother holds her
little girl up to the railing, and asks if she
would like to join them and "go swimming."

Tree toads snap beneath us like branches,
but there are no songbirds here today
to dazzle us with their yellows: wrens, warblers,
goldfinches, vireos have left for the season,
along with Bullock's oriole, bright Halloween orange
of the Western Tanager, and red Grosbeak too.
And where we ask are the promised owls who
are supposed to be raising their young?

Only a harrier marsh hawk flies above us.
No ubiquitous Blue Heron or Bald Eagles fish
on the river as the Nisqually runs quietly past
the high-powered binoculars of the visitors
searching for their river otters; instead, we see
colorful pictures on the signs, study the way a satyr
angelwing butterfly first cuts, then sews leaves back
together with silk and thread, like a little tailor.

COFFEE HAS TAKEN AWAY THE SONGBIRDS

Coffee has taken away the songbirds
where music held sway in the trees,
land surrendered to hard economics,
agro where there once was shade,
sun has filled in the fields.

Silence has become profitable,
increasing yield as the earth throws up
its coffee beans, a sky of harvest
but robbed of its grace, no traces
of open-mouthed warblers for us.

Look in your next cup,
you will not see their nests,
but somewhere in the treetops
they will be singing of new buds
without this bitter aftertaste.

WORDS REMOVED FROM THE OXFORD
JUNIOR DICTIONARY 12 YEARS AGO

It's been 12 years since
the last *acorn* fell
and the *adder* struck again,
the *bluebell* is languishing
and the *dandelion* gone to seed.

The *sword fern* is still dangling
and the *heron's* drooping wings,
the crest of the *kingfisher*
has lost its crown.
The *newt* and *salamander* gone.

And now, under the missing *willow*
tree, the smithy no longer stands,
his *horseshoe* luck run out
near where the *otter* disappeared
for good down the river's mouth.

MONDEGREEN

Memory makes of us brief cameos.
   —Sharon Hashimoto

Memory makes of us Grief canoes,
a place of cedar wishes
where we hollow out the mind,
a place to live and move
in the current of our words
that pass us—as we row
parallel with the shore.

Holding our paddles tight
as we cross hand over hand
in camaraderie again and press
our prose in grief to make
the heartwood move, the crown
of our being a knot
that no one can replace.

SONNET BOX

If I wanted to lock myself into a frame,
the place would be inside a sonnet box—
a wooden form from which no sound comes,
a crypt like Poe's for the living dead,
a place that springs shut like a mousetrap
where I can rest the jewel of my head
and hold my breath in eerie silence
releasing only a caesura at a time.

Like the puff of a filter cigarette,
just enough to let someone know that
I live under cover of an oak casket.
Inside I sip an extra dry vermouth,
never bother anyone with the truth,
make a point to keep my mouth shut.

BOOKWORM

"Excuse us, the snails have eaten your mail"
—British Postal Service

A book made of cardboard
filled in cracks with words
and tied with string, a braid
or two words pasted on the cover
Like Water to the Moon
opens like the heart's secret chambers.

I find your words a solace
against the rain, turning
another page waiting for the eye
to settle its wandering, always looking
to rest, knowing words are like breath.

You must take them in, hold them
in your chest awhile before you exhale
and find release again—
and sometimes if you look,
tucked into the corner like the mail—
a tiny snail.

III.

HOLY LANDS
Mediterranean to the Black Sea

At the Round Earth's imagined corners, blow

—John Donne, *Holy Sonnet 7*

ROAD TO A GRECIAN URN

Here lies One Whose Name was writ in Water.
  —Keats' grave, Protestant Cemetery, Rome

In Rome, I walked over water,
the Tiber had shriveled up, I paced
while waiting at the cemetery door.
The gates were locked until 3 o'clock.

A man with puppy-dog eyes tried
to pick me up, not flattering myself,
I think it was an Italian film director
but brushed him off as gently as I could.

I found the Pyramid of Cestius with a map,
the nearby grave of Severn, buried with
his children; then Keats next to him.
The sun had barely given its shade.

I waited there an hour for One Whose
Name was writ in Water, my thirst was slaked.
I placed a tiny stone on his grave
white as the blue-veined marble itself.

A simple headstone marked the spot—
a poet's death—I took my time, sat down
nearby, no one there now for me to wait on
but *him*. The solace of a poet's life.

LEDA AND THE SWAN IN POMPEII

Uncovered in a cubiculum:
a fresco on the wall
where Leda is unearthed,
gazing out at us in thrall,
the swan's white body splayed
across her rose-colored thighs.

Zeus in the act of impregnating,
while Leda accepts her
"swan turn" there to inflame
the passions, a common ploy
and with her we feel the wings.

Beating down on her as Leda with
her cape covers him, a surrogate
birth and so is all beauty made
a servant, burnished and tarnished
as though a flame had died.

YOUNG MAN READING THE ILIAD

after the painting Youth Transcribing Homer
by Johannes Moreelse

Imagine in the creases
intense fields of war, is he
Hector summoning up his army?

For in the narrow wooden face,
I see his profile on a coin,
his modelled modern face.

He is turning the pages—
re-reading the old glory,
I see him squinting back

to the Trojan War, full of blood
before the war was born,
when Helen was only a woman.

HAĠAR QIM

The snail-like shells,
boats in a harbour of rocks
in the shadows of the sun
where wind says its mantra,
and holes in the stone open
our eyes to these "keyholes."

Snails crawl from these shells.
May St. Paul bless this little fleet
as I dip hands in this holy water
and sing of these stones,
ripples form in these rocks,
the soft light in pores breathe in
dust from these poems.

MDINA, THE SILENT CITY

You will see people at a distance
but no one will answer your prayers,
you rest at the Door of the Dolphins
on the steps of the cathedral,
wind moaning some old lullaby.
Your mind is your temple.

It keeps saying, "Don't make waves."
Only the ghost of the carthorse
making its rounds, an empty dungeon
echoes of plague and inquisition.
Where the moon guides your path,
love has no word for death.

MY COMINGS AND GOINGS FROM MOSTA

A Jesus with light bulbs rises
from the ruins of a petrol station
and the rotunda of the dome.

Today we go to Marsaxlokk,
the fishing village and market.
Is it in my dream?

Mary, Jesus, and Joseph encased
in their plastic aquarium
above the driver's head, look down

from their bubble. We head for Valetta
to the hack of diesel fumes,
pass churches shaped like pinecones,

flowering hibiscus by the roadside
while we drive in the shade,
hoping the road will be our way.

Our father who drives in shadow,
here we must be close to heaven.
The driver ratchets down the gears,

while passengers who stand holding
prayer ropes bow their heads
as we drive through valleys of rocks

past palm trees and cactus, hanging
from a thread like the head of St. John
waiting to be severed from this landscape,

like the canvas of Caravaggio sent
back to Italy to be repaired. May
we be mended. Spare us.

Hollow be our names, if we could
we'd lie down in green pastures,
but on Malta it isn't allowed.

Here, there are Jehovah's Witnesses,
time shares sold on the harbour,
our bones bleach white as limestone.

How much we take for granted,
the bomb that fell through the dome
here at Mosta and never exploded.

People here don't lock their doors,
knowing someone is watching when
they're not home.

KAYMAKLI UNDERGROUND CITY

It's like being a coal miner—
I bend over into the tunnel core,
cold air and quiet, dead still air.
I am alone, having escaped sitting
on a rock I hope is not sacrificial.

Each pore opens, the spores grow
inside me, like being inside a bone
living in the eye-socket of the earth's
the occipital lobe. Or peristalsis.

Here it's like a mosque, I can rest,
find peace while travelling
for so long; here I sit on any
worry stone while voices come and go.

Following me in English and Turkish,
a mixture sweet as opium;
there are humans in these stones,
deep in the marrow I have come.

For all those who lived here
no central heating, no sun or light
could have entered this hollow place—
fibrous rock, stale air, and dust.

Electric lights only illuminate
the dampness that clings like sod.
Pigeonholes, millstones fill these
catacombs. Whoever lived here
breathed deeply.

JAMELA, 2005

She lives in sacrifice to the smoke of the burning dump,
and so when she asked me to bring her cigarettes, I
said, "What brand?"
    —Keith Shawe, *A Portrait of the Roma of*
        Southern Macedonia

As though she had a white goat's beard,
the smoke curls around her chin.
She in a black headscarf, a rock herself,
face black as a coal miner's devil,
she puffs in contrast to the white cigarette
plume, ghost of the quarry of her garbage dump
that she mines for metal and plastic.

Goya could not have improved on her,
deep hollows of her cheeks, pits for eyes.
A face in total eclipse, a forehead creased.
Did she answer from the sand-filled
windpipes, rasping a cough from
the dead oasis that would kill a camel?
She turns her head, becomes her shadow.

FATA MORGANA AT PAMUKKALE

"Cotton Castle" in Turkish

Here in the desert
you find an oasis in white robes,
a miracle of cascading stones
washes through the carbuncle of your ear,
and warm continuously flowing
water from underground springs.

Pools everywhere, steppingstones,
while you enter the green water
seeming to stand on the edge
of a waterfall, cliffs of limestone,
looking into the valley below,
standing in a slough of soft minerals.

Pamukkale, an inland beach,
a Roman spring from the ancient baths
still warming you with men and women
bathing beauties—all of you reveling
like the blond-haired Germans and
the dark-eyed Italians, everyone sitting
on the edge looking down at Eden.

THE WINDMILLS OF HYDRA

The windmills of Hydra
sit like sinister spiders,
the great Peloponnese Coast
casts its shadows
while a Turner sun reflects
the Saronic Gulf as I
drink my morning coffee.

Donkey bells call to evening
below the monastery,
one man Greek,
one Italian woman
take a wheelbarrow
down to the water.
The windmills of Hydra
spin like sinister spiders.

A Greek salad for Madame Maria
with tomatoes, cucumber, olive,
feta cheese and Greek coffee.
The cicadas sing that we live
among brothers; meanwhile
the windmills of Hydra
sing like sinister spiders.

BOSPHORUS

Here it is calming.
In good time I will leave,
but now with the wind
at my back and pastel light

and the umbrellas ballooning
like jellyfish, I can sit
and watch the water traffic:
harbor boats, tankers, tourist ships
in the seeing eye of the distant

minarets, the dome of Hagia Sofia
and the Blue Mosque, a tanker
from Yugoslavia, and then to separate
the masts across to the Asian side.

For here on the western side, nearing
sunset, it's quite enough for reflection.
I have leisure to stare at the graveyard
under the spell of the Pashas.

READING *ISTANBUL: MEMORIES AND THE CITY* BY ORHAN PAMUK

My coffee-stained book
in black and brown print—
smudges of my fingerprints
powder of coffee beans.
I hear the muezzin calling
from his tower, orisons
as we go to *ground*.

Framed on pages, engravings
rise from the Bosphorus
Yalis, along the shores
a windblown chorus of dogs
sing of the old harem
at Topkapi Palace, those
ornate rooms, Ottoman skies.

Over the roofs and minarets,
the innumerable mosques
and Grand Bazaar, warrens
and hammams slapping
with the sound of human flesh,
silver tea pouring down.

I pray to the East, I pray
to the west—to the humble
basket bearers, bent-double
under their burden, to the beggar
in rags who lives in the open,
the shadow of his shroud,
to a Byzantium of clouds.

MY PHONE CARD FROM MARRAKECH

for Caryl Ward

My phone card from Marrakech
has the mandala of Marrakech
in sea-blue waves of Arabic,
dots that make small faces
where writing is a practiced art
and Moorish arches hold up
the pediment of sky.

Here wind will devour you.
It will speak to you of time,
no sand in your hourglass,
grains of vision so fine
they rub in your eye to become
a pearl of your sight.

When you call home
you are so far away, friends
will imagine they hear a voice.
In La Place Djemaa El Fna,
the charmers will have worked
their magic so that even the snakes
won't hang up.

TWO EPIGRAMS

for Karim

I.

To polish the mirror,
smooth vanity of paper.
To touch the place
of your visage
without blinking
is the truth of
your making.

II.

The sky is written in Arabic,
the clouds in poetry.
Prose is the Rock of Gibraltar.
Earth is our mother,
our father is the sea.

AVIARY, DOLMBAHÇE PALACE

From Yorkshire to Australia
the canaries are singing,
the prize peacock parading
while females wait in their wisdom.

So much song-making,
they almost drown out
the sirens at midday droning
the muezzin over the loudspeaker.

These Turkish women are shy
but you cannot wait too long,
you may not have another life
worth singing for.

BLANK VERSUS

My face keeps staring out this window
longing for another face, a Cycladic sculpture,
a narrow bridge of the nose perhaps
from Rodos, sundial face, no hour written
on it yet, the minutes' muse moves like flies,
keeps falling off, leaving smooth surface
ready for it to pass: Adriana of Naxos,
Helen of Troy, Lydia of Persepolis,
or maybe Eurydice in Hades. As I look
back, trying to rest my eyes at last
in the sleeping cradle of the moon, I find
words that are, after all, my saving grace.

ATTRITION

Slowly I replace what's lost,
my walking shoes worn through
in Istanbul
have now turned into Turkish slippers,
and still I walk on sandals
from the Black Village, Karaköy
where I visited the brothels.

The marble road to Ephesus, polished
smooth by the feet of tourists' shoes
down the corridor of trees
and into pools of Pamukkale that overflow
cascades of waterfalls wash our pilgrim
feet clean again, between our toes.

Sunglasses left behind me in the bus
station at Ürgüp will shade a Turkish man's
eyes from such temptations I could only
imagine in the Harem at Topkapi Palace.
There is little left I cannot lose.

But what has been given back?
Fig trees are for picking, the apples
and there are oranges and bananas
growing outside Antalya and Göreme.
Eat and leave the rest behind
for others to find.

At Xanthos, rest your feet in the colosseum
where I visited the Harpies monuments
and at the border between Greece
and Turkey where I saw storks nesting
on the tops of telephone poles.

Somewhere in Thessalonica, a Greek
walks to the football stadium in my sandals.
In Ürgüp, a Turk sees through my glasses,
and in Istanbul, the shoes I left behind
may be on the feet of a basket bearer
doubled over even now, giving
thanks to Allah.

IV.

LIMELIGHT
Last Calls and Final Acts

*I watch dusk descend like a poem
in the pale light...of the streetlamps.*

—Orhan Pamuk,
Istanbul: Memories and the City

LIMELIGHT

In the pale yellow circle of this lamp
on a pinewood table full of knots,
under a plain white ceiling stretched
like a sheet, this body unprotected,
I have come to talk, with no one
to keep me company but my Lettera 37.

Here I can tell my secrets, command
a space, and make even these walls
listen, while the bed creaks above
from the people in the flat making love.
My answer to them has only the sound
of a typewriter's quick strokes.

Before those lights go out at ten
and birds begin to nest in the eaves
just before it's time to start once more,
to take new pecking orders, I know the lines:
it's time to rehearse, come center stage,
once again to fill the room with characters.

AUDITION

I'm here at Pinewood Studios
wearing my sexy shoes
and my crooked, gap-toothed smile
waiting for an audition to play
a real stiff or a lady-killer.

They're all here: Peter Sellers,
Alec Guiness, the Lavender Hill
Mob, and I'm baby-faced Nelson,
teeth full of bullets, I know how to
carry a .38 tucked in my pocket.

The only question is—do I have
the right stuff, the Bermondsey
look, the smell of the South Thames?
Can I tail my own shadow
and never get caught?

HABEAS CORPUS

Leaving the sentence lying like a torso
on its side.
          —Graham Greene

Leave it then, half-finished,
fingered like a profile ¾ view
half a nose, one eye, a lip
imagining what the other side
of the moon is like, rough draft
of a face, fact, or fiction. Picasso?

What is hidden from view—
unsettling it's true, but artistic license
is needed here, means you can be
both judge and jury too, filling in
the missing pieces, a corpse
with clues that don't lie flat.

IT SHOULD HAVE BEEN JOSEPH COTTEN

Suddenly there he is in his overcoat
rakish hat, carrying a valise,
a little of Holly Martens in mid-stream.
A silly name Anna Schmidt says,
or from "Duel in the Sun"
the good McCanles son.

Always a decent man, genteel,
well-spoken, eager to please,
buy you a drink, as Caspar Gutman
said in the Maltese Falcon,
genuine coin of the realm.

He is still walking in that corridor
of trees, the long panning shot
where Valli walks away from him,
the final shot where in the end,
with the right cast, he gets the girl
—at last.

FILM NOIR

From your hotel room the spider lines crisscross outside
and moonbeams signal a crescent in the sky above Vienna
as the constellation of the Riesenrad turns another notch.
On the other side of the Danube, there are excavations,
giant cranes holding up their scaffolds, ready to prop up
buildings on another set; these are the new erections.

On the nearby Joseph Strasse, Klimt lived
and painted society women, while upstairs Mozart
fathered The Magic Flute. The circular Ringstrasse
revolves and the empire of Franz Josef shows
its decorous front, the Kunst Museum displays
embellishments of Lapis Lazuli, gold trimmings
and crystal bowls: Royal Lipizzans prance
at the Spanish Riding School to the gentry's applause.

Here, men walk stiff legged as Prussians with upturned
collars and fat women hike their skirts, sunning
themselves on park benches, while sex shops remain
hidden behind their two-way mirrors.
The merchants from the diamond stores eye
you coolly as detectives, guessing at your business:
the story is you are here for keepsakes—
the rumors fly north, south, east,
and west to every zone.

Narrow side streets lead to a theatre where
"The Third Man" plays its final scenes, Holly Martens
walking away from his destiny with Anna,
Freud's couch and castration dreams leading you
into blind alleys, mysterious women seem to follow
you, while enormous men in overcoats
expose themselves, airing their bellies

in Votive Park, and down the maze of streets
come thundering one-eyed streetcars, the cyclops.

The clock strikes, dogs bark, you wait in
the cell of your room, tomorrow you leave for
Czechoslovakia, tonight you sweat out
the numbered hours, this city of monumental
darkness, as empty streets lead you to reflect:
there will be a border crossing, a passport check.
They will hold your visa in the palm of their hands,
but tonight you lie awake waiting for
the false dawn all the way to Prague.

SLAVIA CAFÉ, PRAGUE, 1984

after the painting The Absinthe Drinker
by Viktor Oliva

Closing time; a new moon lingers, Venus
resting in her cradle, and in the painting
an old man sits at his table watching a
mermaid flick the lovely tail she tries to hide.

The old gentleman smiles, meanwhile, the waiter
stands pigeon-toed who lives in a visible world
where an empty bottle, a glass half-filled means
he's ready to leave. It's closing time.

The lovers have drifted away two by two,
below swans are fishing on the Vltava,
its old name before the Moldau, and the spirit
of Smetana sleeps in the churchyard.

Above, the Castle Hradčany keeps its distance,
St. Vitus Cathedral, a silhouette in spires,
while Charles Bridge links the old and lesser
towns of Prague, none figures in his memory.

Only the Green Lady, gazing through him in this
painting while he stares, the music plays
until she disappears for bad, for good,
slipping away to leave him on these rocks.

THE MARIONETTES OF PRAGUE

With their proud painted faces
staring out of the window—
through mascara and rouge,
nimbly quick, spindle foot,
they dance to a fiddle tune.

In the Jewish quarter—
stones piled on the graves
in tribute next to the only
synagogue spared by Hitler—
we are witness to
the art of the lost children.

Next, Russian tanks rolled
into Wenceslas Square, puppets
flinched at the gunfire,
learned new steps to dance,
as the Moldau flowed on
underneath the Red Star.

Now when we see their faces,
regard these children of tears,
those who fought for freedom
dance with wooden legs
to their own strings above,
the Vltava on Charles Bridge.

CHIAROSCURO

In the back streets of Havana
two boys are dangling their legs
like fishing poles, their shadows
look like herons as the light
spreads dust on tiles shining
as if they were freshly scrubbed.

The ornamental iron
spreads its fanlike spokes while
the sun wheels above. Someone
is pouring water from a vase
like they were in a medina,
here their grotty marketplace.
Pencil in their brothers, sisters.
Make it charcoal.

POINTLESS

The French are all gangsters
at heart, like Jean Paul Belmondo
with a smoking cigar, blowing off
every chance he gets.

Jean Seberg, a striped zebra
in her turtleneck sweater—
it's useless to protest,
not with that smile like an impala.

And his cauliflower ears,
the pug-ugly nose of a fighter
as they romp through Montmartre
at night, not quite sure

who their enemies are,
stealing cars, killing a cop,
smoking Gauloises, falling asleep
in each other's arms.

He runs down the street,
six slugs in his back,
her dulcet eyes, his derelict hat,
her pouting lips as she watches
his eyes tighten to the close-up.

Life is really a bitch when
you're French and black and white,
before color came along
and ruined the night.

MURDER WEAPON

It is the silent word
that threatens us,
the polished word
sticking in our throats.

All hint at violence:
the inward-looking glance,
the holes in the ellipsis...
a bulge beneath the overcoat.

All show just enough
to make you sense the instrument,
ill-defined, but poised,
point-blank.

NIGHTWATCH

Every night it comes to trouble me,
when I am half-asleep, it breathes.
Its breath creeps up my rigid spine.
While my eyelids are still trembling,
it stalks me to the corners of my room,
daring me to take my fill of dreams.

I know that creature better than myself,
it lingers close, waiting to be seen,
like the exhibitionist in the window,
he knows I cannot help looking at him,
to see the naked thing, stark and unashamed,
that blank face locked inside the carriage.

Face to face, we wait the moment out,
until the beads of type begin to rise,
popping out along its pale forehead,
until I strike it blow on ringing blow,
the air chatters with my quick strokes,
and my fingers weaken and fall limp.

My rising pulse returns to normal.
Nothing moves; the air is quiet again.
There it lies before me on the table,
cold and frail beneath the moonlight,
marks still fresh, the lacerated skin
is corpse stiff in my imagination.

WATCHING DA VINCI'S INQUEST

In the murky dark, somewhere beneath the pier
a body washes up. *We got a floater here.*
What is your story? What can you tell us?
Da Vinci talks to corpses, you see—

The coroner's job is to speak for the dead.
Her eyes still open. *She's not a jumper.*
They put her in a body bag like tobacco
zip-lock, then haul the body back

to the pathologist's dissecting table.
Vancouver is #1 in overdoses in North
America, he says, as they wheel the gurney
across the glossy floor like a wheelbarrow.

The parent shows up, "Why won't they
release the body?" *Because there's a*
baby inside, Da Vinci says, *and this complicates*
matters, since a baby doesn't ingest heroin.

Da Vinci, a case in himself, walks a crooked
line straight through Chinatown where he
drinks his fill of whiskey, has bad dreams
as they find the grayest house in Vancouver,

white trim. A man with a simian face opens
the door, they go inside, find heroin in a talcum
powder container. *That is what the baby licked*
to end the short episode of his life.

ORPHEUS AND EURYDICE RETOLD

by Christoph Willibald Gluck, performed by
Chicago Lyric Opera and Robert Joffrey Ballet

She dies in a dark place
her car crashed, wrapped around a tree,
and I, without her, Orpheus, pick up the pieces
of her photographs, depart so out of tune,
I carry her shroud to hear her voice
once more aloud, the silence keep her
spirit that I may sing to her again.

What can I do but find the natural world,
may winds carry her prayer and proper
the windows black without her, Eurydice,
her ghost in a white, white dress
so her name is carved in darkness.
You gods bring her back to me now.

So I may go to the underworld accompanied
by Charon and Pluto. Deliver her to me!
As I, a poet, may go to find her, win her back
against all tyrants, may she return my bride.
I play my sweetest lyre against all tyrants.
May she return my bride, so I see a ray
of light, as her faithful husband I must never
look at her, or she'll be lost to me forever.

Decreed by Jupiter, that I must obey
to not look on her sweet face,
and so, I will win her back to me
but I must never look back at her
or my head will roll, my eyes with tears
can't bring her back to see that lovely face!
The birds will sing what I cannot sing.

O spirits, I plead with you
to see the demons of my torment, and so I
carry her photograph to remind me
of her lovely face! I show you what I'm looking for.
So carry me to her distress! I soften you
with my music and enchanting words
as I go to Hades to bring her back. O, Eurydice!
I cannot find you except by my voice!
I look for you, a man alone without a looking glass.

SARAH VAUGHN SINGING "YOU'D BE SO NICE TO COME HOME TO"

London House, Chicago, 1958

Hearing her voice, gates gently swing
in that silky way, the lioness herself with
all that beautiful sassiness, makes you want
to as soon as possible—I mean—get home!

With her beside you on the couch,
happy just to hear her sing, Sarah,
with her brightness and the lovely phrasing
made just for you. How nice it would be

in the middle of a pandemic when you're tired
of rewriting to hear something original—
instead of a buzz feed! A message just

for you with horn flirtation accompaniment
to adjust to, just the two of you and the
orchestra—all alone—in London House.

THE VOICE IN THE MACHINE

for my wife, Jean

As a child I used to sing *Be My Love*
as though I was Mario Lanza—
hiding behind the living room sofa
to serenade my parents in my childish tenor.
And with my kisses set you burning
straining for the highest notes, trying
to be true to the voice of the master or
whoever else would listen, *that I adore.*

All the while the Capitol Dome on the label
kept spinning around in the background
with a purple sky I wanted to fly around
until I was too dizzy for love of the record
machine in my voice to turn it off; and it
kept spinning like the wheel of fortune until
I knew, *eternally—that you—will be my love!*

STAR QUALITY

for J.M.

I love your lion's mane,
how you wear it like mink
around your shoulders.
The green glow in your eyes
and then the close-up.

Just bathing in your iris,
I can float for days,
watching the setting sun
or see the phases of the moon
played out in cameo roles.

Your head rests easily
in the palm of my shoulder,
like your breasts in my hands.
You make little noises
that break into choruses.

The curtain comes down
late at night and I am in
your dressing room at last,
after the show, still waiting
for your autograph.

THE CIRCUS

After we have slapped our thighs
once more and we laugh quietly
down in the pit of our bellies,
there will be tougher acts to follow—
clown-face, white-face, lovers.
We could walk on our hands,
see the big-top go spinning
or rolling over like lions,
lie on our backs yawning.

With love as our ringmaster
and three rings going at once,
who would know what to watch,
our extraordinary juggling act
where I suspend you, breathless,
cupped in the palms of my hands,
or the thrills of the high wire
as we touch briefly, passing again,
tempting luck and death,
losing our balance only for fun
before we come down to earth.

Or me on the burning trapeze,
you my star-spangled accomplice
dressed only in a handkerchief
as we perform our triple somersault.
And finally, our sweeping bows,
followed of course by applause,
the cotton candy and hoopla,
the horns and glittering girls,
spotlights swinging above our heads
as we exit through the roof.

MAIN ATTRACTIONS

They dance in air, on Chinese
fire poles, shimmying to the top,
shimmering aerialists performing
their escapes in white jump suits.

Clowns with long Italian noses
and Commedia Dell'arte harlequins,
Pantelone, the red-haired woman,
the dancer, the star-spangled pony.

Two strong men, all joint and muscle,
balance each other in counterpoint
under the white egg-shell circus
sky of *Cirque de Soleil*.

A swinging rope ladder drops down
like a cobra from above our heads
while acrobats launch themselves
like cannonballs into the darkness.

A woman juggles a waterfall,
and two bolo dancers circumscribe
the air in arcs to syncopated heels
that go rat-a-tat-tat.

After intermission, a man from
the crowd comes up on stage
to fight a mute gun battle
with one of the clowns.

Spider men sidle down their threads
in front of us, then fly back up,
exchanging places on their platforms,
execute mid-air passes overhead.

Next to me, they're fastening the lunges,
and a drum beat pounds out the finale.
After the clowns have taken their bows,
everyone appears on stage.

We sit clasping each other's hands,
as they rush to their final exits.
We rise wondering what to do next,
with the ground so firmly beneath us.

AT INTERMISSION (NOT TOM STOPPARD)

The little girls sit on each
other's laps; our hands so
tightly bound like their pony
tails, finally come undone.

And the smiling couple next to us,
so sure that I am the playwright,
and his wife, pass us, nod
"Thank you!" happy to have met us.

I have something to say to you
that touches us; I am not
the man they thought I was,
and you are not my wife.

Instead, things have changed,
before the bell goes to call us back
I have something to say to you,
"I want you to be my wife."

When we return, the little girls
sleep on each other's shoulders,
the smiling couple look to each other,
at the new couple sitting next to them.

STILL LIFE

after "West Central Park, New York City,"
a photo by Gordon Gilbert

The sun, a white moon
in the scant trees where I'd like
to be sitting on one of the benches,
book open, reading the light
on my page, significant shadows
reach out across the pavement.

The coded streetlamps wait
for something to appear in
the censor, but everything is still,
heads bowed, legs crossed, spaced apart
without a comma fault
in ones and twos, solos and duets
studying their parts.

OBITUARY: THE DEATH OF INSPECTOR MORSE

Obituary: John Thaw is dead at 60,
played TV's Inspector Morse

You, of all people, who loved
your liquor and your women full-bodied—
even if they didn't always love you!
You raced through the Oxford countryside
in your red Jag to the sound of Wagner.

With a claret jug, you hated the sight
of blood. "Unseemly Morse," said Inspector Strange.
"Strange—strange in manner," you said. But
when you died in real life it seemed like a relative
had gone to ground—much to our remorse.

The drunken one, intellectual uncle who stroked out.
How I'll miss the clear blue eyes, eagle's crown.
We're left like Sergeant Lewis to puzzle, daub
our eyes with a tissue of clues, the classic ones—
now you've solved the ultimate crossword.

THEY LIVE BY NIGHT

It's getting dark
and the lovers are fleeing.
Keechie and Bowie
look through the window while
the road recedes in white unbroken lines
that keep turning away,
like this page forever in the middle
of nowhere where trees rise up in rage.

The two lovers are leaning into
each other, side-by-side pressing against
the steering wheel, her head on his
shoulder as they head off somewhere—
where everywhere looks the same.
It's getting darker now, though at times
the white lines come at them like bullets

they must dodge, as he takes the turn
then straightens again as his hands covet
the steering wheel, and Keechie stirs
to say something while Bowie drives,
their lives crazy as he speeds off
into the night where she can sleep safely,
letting go of his eyes in the rear-view mirror.

POETIC LICENSE PLATE

Ahead of me a license plate—
BOYD138, illuminating me.
But he's not driving anymore,
his body donated to science,
his eyes for someone else to see.

I realized Boyd, my father's name
is an anagram for body
who art somewhere I am not,
still persists in my memory
his smile in the rear-view mirror.

I feel he's been driving away
for years, I'd like to follow him
down the road show him how
well I can parallel park, and how
I drive defensively after dark.

But wish I could keep his name
in front of me, that his name,
my middle name could go on,
but I have no children, just
a name written in headlights.

NIGHT MAILMAN

for my Father

At night, I take off my mask,
I walk the hallowed ground
under streetlights, where I meet no one,
past the broken noses of the lions
and swimming sea turtles across
the street, cross over the crosswalk,
don't let the curbs trip me up,
on the lawns of well-kept citizens who
keep secrets no one listens to,
down alleys with long-legged shadows
where potholes don't follow me,
making sure I am always alone.

Make my rounds where no one's home,
a night mailman, nothing to deliver
in my close-mouthed pouch, skip
over addresses in my book, holding
cards no one sent, keeping track of
all dead letters that I will return
to be re-cased and re-sorted for
the living, unceremoniously
yet to be delivered, my sack is growing,
my bag is aching, still I can't begin
to tell you of these words, forgotten.
What I couldn't find, I carry with me
for another time, when I'll return
after the daylight sounds.

BEDTIME STORY

At night, he would come to sit on my bed,
my father filling my head with flying dreams
of horses as his voice coaxed me into listening.
I believed everything—the cattle rustlers
who escaped, chased by helicopters,
their blades whirling like gales up the gulch,
and when they rushed from Montana across
the border into Canada, I fled too, spooked
like a Canada goose, with my head laid back
on the run, fugitive from my father's arms,
hunted by the Mounties on horseback,
free and wild as the cattle thieves and rustlers
until he hugged me, hugged me hard,
told me how their campfires alerted the lawmen
and led to where they hid in the trees.

Sparks flew, wind carried the message back
so that even as they slept, the Mounties circled them
while the bandits snored, dreaming of getaways
and cattle cars that filled trains clear to Chicago.
And I thought I was safe, too, when he kissed me
and said good night, leaving me to lie there
my head full of posses, the sleeping outlaw gang
and dreaming of new exploits my father hadn't yet
told me, the ones he always left hanging
like the noose that always awaited the outlaws.
Now, he's gone. Where, even he can't tell me.
Those ghost riders have crossed the night in songs
so many times, their fires are cold, the trail gone.
He's left only me behind to tell his story.

V.

PILGRIMAGE
Scotland and England

*Together the youth and the old man were to
read the world's horoscope.*

—Shirley Hazzard, *Transit of Venus*

AT THE TEMPLE OF THE GLEN, IONA

The arrowhead points to eloquence,
down the trough of the valley
to the Irish Sea, look towards the cleft
in the hills, the hay lying in hazy furrows,
formed in a zigzag pattern like the chevrons
at Newgrange that gave the rocks new words.

Down the throat to the Irish Sea
where Spouting Rock shoots up like a geyser,
the center rock dividing the valley like tonsils,
I stand here on this Rock of Oratory
with no whiskey to age my words.
I throw my voice toward America like Marconi did
from Mizen Head across the Atlantic, in a code
yet to be broken—hoping you'll hear.

MINDING THE GAP

At the platform, a girl practices
her "Riverdancing" steps, elevating
then kicking out at the darkness
as the headlight beam approaches slowly,
the four fifty-five on time calling
at: *Alfreton, Langley Mills, Long Eaton,*
Nottingham, Grantham, Peterborough,
Ely, Attenborough, and Norwich.

As we leave the crooked spire
of Chesterfield, tilting at windmills
or as lore has it, the devil
bending over to look at the only
virtuous girl in town, across the sky
a neon sign in red, the letters
bleeding "Chesterfield College"
into the sunset.

I read of Mike Tyson's defeat,
and more sleaze in the Tory party,
follow the bushy eyebrows of Michael Heseltine
raising over civil servants and wonder
where on earth the person on the other end
of the mobile phone is calling from.
Is it Whitehall or Taiwan?

As we pass the Trinity open coal site,
the track is jumping, dropping a stitch,
in this tunnel of night we count
our blessings, the coach warm as a tea cosy.
We have no rebels or Tutsis to fight.
Ahead is only the platform at Alfreton,
a colliery pit from which no man shines.

Red poppies have wilted by now, delivering us
from Remembrance Day, having kept the peace
for two minutes, we congratulate ourselves
at having done our level best, but feel
the weightiness of damp air in our lungs,
counting lights going past above our heads.
We ghosts of British rail, dreaming as we ride
of a home we can't see, beyond the dead.

CULLODEN BATTLEFIELD

Here where the moors are parted like fresh-cut hay,
the Scottish clans were slaughtered
by Butcher Cumberland in 1746, while
Bonnie Prince Charlie fled in his disguise.

Among these gray stones and cairn clan graves
marked "mixed clan" or "Campbell" or "MacDougall"
or some other name our lips grow cold on—
we have come here to stand over these dead.

Whether they were burned in barns or hacked
to bits, the sorrows all the same; I must not trouble
them, I see the faces of the living, they look as white
as mine near the well of the dead.

A dripping forest, T-allt Ruah, the burn rises in
my blood where MacGillivray the regiment commander
is buried, and I see a redeeming rainbow
carve the sky above my head.

I feel for those who could not run.
Today is penny bright, but where the shadows are
I leave behind my sympathy in footprints,
where the colors stained, the stones bled.

CLASS PHOTO: CHILDREN OF DUNBLANE

Those excited faces are now frozen in time.
Look at the shoulders squeezed forward; hands clasped
stiff-armed at the lap—expressions of pure joy.
    —Seattle Times editorial

We need to remember you with eyes wide open,
your sweet smiles and glad looks
you gave to your teacher, and to hold
you forever at this moment of hope.

No one spoke after it was over,
your bodies piled in the corner like skip ropes.
Instead, we want to remember the girl who said
six "good-byes" to her mother at the gate.

For the rest of us still left standing,
knowing now that so few escaped, tell us,
please, this is only a bad nursery rhyme.
Give us an ending even adults can believe in.

ARTHUR'S SEAT

The shell of sky opens to pearl
above Edinburgh,
a city of shells scattered over my eye
to the right of Calton Hill,
the masthead of Nelson's monument,
the cannon aimed towards Princes Street
and tourists, the palace a crown of granite,
a sheer wall where Queen Mary's baby
was lowered by rope from her cell window
to escape the wrath of an English Queen.

I sit on a rock, herding the clouds
with only my eye to tend these gothic spires.
I say *Amen* to this bad weather,
my head bowed against the wind
where Scott, Burns, Stevenson
came as rightful heirs to climb this
"Flight of Arrows" to an archer's throne.

I have only my eyes and words
to tell you of these prayers I know,
the sky that opens like a dome,
thickets of rain, shafts or rainbows,
this heap of rocks I stand upon bareheaded
to deliver this sermon out of stone
before all the silver of Edinburgh,
to a city that is not my own.

THE COWS AS MONOLITHS

This monument is in the care
of the Ministry of Works.
It is an offense to injure or deface it.

Here at Arbor Low Stone Circle, they can still be seen,
descendants of the Bronze Age to the present day.
Observe how they keep their positions in the grass,
how when it's raining, they kneel, or when it's clear
appear to be standing, silhouetted against the sky.

No one knows how they came, why to them
this ground is holy; ever since we've been here,
they've been watching us but still have not moved
nor made a sound. In the foreground a sheepdog lies,
waiting for its calling, while still frozen the cows keep
their monumental silence in black and white.

Nearby, we see a ditch with two entrances, a henge.
"A round barrow is built over the bank," the sign says.
The rest dismantled in antiquity, now only
they remain still grazing in a farmer's field
near Derbyshire. Here we see them in this photograph
to the present day: still, untouched.

MARKED BY A PALM

for Peggy Anne

I am the hummingbird etched
in the stone, drawn
to your flower, my cousin
I have come to stand over you
in the sun, without words,
to kneel in the grass
because it has been so long.

A witness to your face
I hold before me, the mirror
of the "laughing place" we went to
as children to tell stories
to each other in the dark.
Do you remember? Are you
listening to still another?

Are you practicing random kindness,
those senseless acts of beauty
that you loved to quote? Consider,
for a moment, this single palm
where the lines run out as I
am writing this letter to you:
this space we keep in touch.

SATURNALIA

On Saturnalia, this day of hiding,
I recede like the sun among
the wreath and holly I keep inside
my room, with Christmas overflowing.
I pick up my pen again to make
a garland linking words together
to see if I can find my voice,
dormant now, with chanting over
the graves of my mother and wife.
I wonder who is listening?
Do my words dissolve in grass?
What else will I raise from the dead?
Who else can I bring to life?

CHRISTMAS AT LINCOLN, ENGLAND

The mulled wine still simmers
with spices as I climb
to the top of Lincoln hill,
past the cathedral to

the open-air market
where shaggy bells ring
in the cold, and snow
cakes on my boots.

Horns blend in high and
low tones to round my
frozen fingers with buttery
scones, and I'm full of cheer.

This morning, my bones
knit together, my skin
with a glow from the
far off candle of the sun

to warm the blood
of ancestors who long-deceased,
long-ago, celebrated this
winter solstice.

HUNTERS IN THE SNOW

after the painting by Pieter Brueghel The Elder

Belgium is frozen over
outside the gates of Antwerp.
The hunters are remorseless.
Dogs with tails like scythes
carve a leaden landscape.

Geese make iron crosses
in the low, offending sky.
Below, children are skating,
making circles on the ice,
hoping the sun will come back.

The Protestants are hunted
and the humanists haunted
by red emblazoned cardinals
who burn the sites and hang
the heads of scholars high.

Mercator is in Rupelmonde prison
using Gemma's triangulation
to find a way out, until finally
the door opens, and he emerges
into the spring of Flemish fields.

Mercator is lying low working
on his globes, plotting a horizon
line that will join the earth,
both Protestant and Catholic,
a map to make the world whole.

OUT OF SEASON

Winter slows us down toward sleep,
we burrow deep beneath our covers
dreaming of our private season.
We wake each day with weary eyes,
creep out to eat our daily bread,
arrange our collars in the mirror.
Today echoes the day before,
the empty stomach of the fireplace,
the ashes of too many winters.

Outside the life is marginal,
the morning sketched in charcoal,
branches lean as spider webs,
the wind stripping the throat bare,
knifing beneath the collarbone.
We hold the breath inside our lungs
and store up speech like kindling wood.
We stir the coals that flare within.

CITY OF WHISPERS

A man singing to his milk bottle
on the stoop lets his voice ring,
chatting up the world or arguing
with a cow he's never seen.

Another, twitching in his chair,
crossing and uncrossing
his legs, makes up his patter
that spills from the newspaper.

The sane among us barely speak,
sit knees up on buses,
trying to avoid each other's eyes.
We keep our words inside.

But somehow, they escape
past corners of our mouths.
Rumors are only the lies
we tell ourselves.

ROSES IN THE SNOW

Their icy breaths
turn us to frost.
The pink frozen petals
pale as wallflowers
that might have closed if given
half-a-chance, instead
seem to be pouting.

Above, a latticework of branches,
great climbers, these roses,
falling short of safety
bend under the weight of snow,
necks drooping.
Now it's too late
for these stragglers.

Their papery blossoms
will never unfold
their stories, and soon you will
find them at the bottom
of your garden,
their petals broken
like teacups made
from porcelain,
the ones you never mend.

LIKE IRISH GARDENS IN THE RAIN

for Fiona

The smell of lavender,
the red of fuchsia hedges,
all the gentle songs of sparrows
fill up my days
after the meeting of the waters.
Eyes bright as poppies
open before me—

You need to be a singer
and a mourner too
to rise above the sound
of mowers and clippers,
soak in the dirt and dew,
drench your skin and feel.

In your field of vision,
a huge seagull over your
shoulder looks at you,
wondering what you're doing
here, while he's waiting
for lunch. No tea. No crumpets.

KOREAN LULLABY

in honor of Richard O' Neill, 2021
Grammy Winner, Classical Music

Tells of a baby on an island,
as you would cradle your viola
rocking gently on the bridge,
your eyes are shut, my darling
but you hear what in Ireland
might be "O Danny Boy"—
softly, softly, just a toy
you would hold; I strain my bow
to sing of this, a little child,
my eyes are shut: I sing of you
as much, my life I would console.

A REST FROM POETRY

If I think about it, nothing gets done sitting across
looking at the library like a Rubik's Cube,
listening to a Renaissance horn concerto, calling up
Christmas at the door: I think of hanging a wreath to let
someone know "people live here," a few boughs crossed
like palms in hopes flights of angels will descend.

Or at least some drifts of snow, how to begin
recovering from a bout with poetry, the virus
of language entering through every blessed wound
or pore; I'd drink to anyone's health singing out
the old year to keep from picking up this pen,
turning a deaf ear to write an oratorio.

SARAH BRIGHTMAN AND THE PEACOCKS

The peacock thinks she is singing to him
and answers three short cries to his peahen,
while passengers wave from the slow-moving
dinner train to moans of a diesel horn.

Six strong men hold her overhead,
a Diva offering to the Opera gods.
As a bolt of fabric flares like a waterfall,
she climbs her ladder to the moon.

Rising from behind a shimmering curtain
she sings "Nessum Dorma." While suspended
from the ceiling crooning "Nella Fantasia,"
two angels unwind like silkworms.

Her voice, chill and cold as Riesling,
washes down our palates, as she spins
from "Music of the Night" her phantom
prince, a "Requiem" to Andrew Lloyd Webber.

When she sings farewell, "Con Te Partiro,"
the peacocks call again, letting down
their tails to the prima donna, taking encores
they think are coming only to them.

A TRIP TO JERUSALEM

for Peggy and Mike

*Ye Olde Trip to Jerusalem—the oldest pub
in England—1189*

At Glastonbury, the thorn tree brought by Joseph
of Arimathea still flowers at every Christmas,
and Arthur and Guinevere are rumored to be buried
in the Abbey grounds not far from Thor Hill's throne.

And here in Nottingham, the pilgrims still return
to duck their heads beneath the rafters inside the cave,
bending their knees to drink their ale beneath castle walls
while cyclists congregate Saturdays on the lawn.

Crossed swords herald the oldest pub in England,
a sailing ship stuck far from its port circumnavigates
the ceiling halfway on its voyage, rounding now
where the corners curve like a Mercator projection.

Three barmen work in cramped quarters, drawing Bitter,
Guinness, rum and shandy as they pass single file
into the nave, like Magi, for at ships' bells it's known
to every wayfarer that Jerusalem closes her doors.

The pores of sandstone still breathe, weeping pints,
and the treasures of wooden kegs remain sleeping,
as men still finding their legs stumble out across
the horizon to make peace with the sobering world.

A poet comes carrying nothing but his words,
his homage has been paid, he makes his due to drink
in the courtyard, to raise his spirits where journeymen
passed, praying to spy his own journey through a glass.

131

ABOUT THE AUTHOR

Michael Magee's work has been published here, in
England, and in Greece. His poetry has been read
on *The Writer's Almanac with Garrison Keillor* and has
appeared on or been published in *VerseDaily.Org,
Poetry(Chicago), Poetry Northwest, Epoch, PoetryAtlas.Com,
PoetsWest Literary Journal, Staxtes Greek Literary Journal*
and *Riddled with Arrows* and others.

He has read at Shakespeare and Co., Paris, Palace
of the Legion of Honor, and won a First Prize at the
Dancing Poetry Contest in San Francisco. He has also
read on radio for BBC Radio1 and KSER FM PoetsWest.
His play "A Night with Oscar Wilde in Reading Gaol"
was produced in Derby, England and "Shank's Mare"
was made into a movie that won a Best Actor's Prize
at the Script to Screen Bare Bones Film Festival in
Tulsa, Oklahoma.

Magee has been a scriptwriter for dance, movies, radio,
and theatre. He also toured with Billy Smart's Circus in
London, doing publicity and advance work for England's
oldest circus. He currently does publicity work for Open
Sesame, a pop-up art gallery in Tacoma, WA.

Magee was a participant in the 2009 Jack Straw Writer's Program. He received an M.A. in Creative Writing (Poetry) from the University of Washington.

His full-length book *How We Move Toward Light* (MoonPath Press) was published in 2018 and *Cinders of Our Better Angels* by MoonPath Press in 2011. A new chapbook, *Bookends: A Poetic Memoir* was published in July 2021 by LocalGemsPoetryPress.Com. *Self Variations: Travels in Greece and Turkey*, a collection of prose and poetry was published in 2021 by Beaux Arts Press.

Magee volunteers as an Ombudsman for Pierce County Memory Care and lives in Tacoma, Washington.

CPSIA information can be obtained
at www.ICGtesting.com
Printed in the USA
LVHW020421170322
713568LV00007B/625